Rainbows

for Rainy Days

By the same author:

God Knows Your Name

Broken Works Best

Under the Rainbow

Rainbows
for Rainy Days

40 devotional readings that reveal God's promises

Catherine Campbell

MONARCH
BOOKS

Published by Monarch Books
www.lionhudson.com
Part of the SPCK Group
SPCK, 36 Causton Street, London, SW1P 4ST

ISBN 978 0 85721 289 4

Acknowledgments
All Scripture references are taken from the New King James Version of the Bible, unless stated otherwise. Copyright © 1982 by Thomas Nelson, Inc. Used by permission. All rights reserved. Scripture quotations marked "NIV" are taken from the Holy Bible, New International Version, copyright © 1973, 1978, 1984 International Bible Society. Used by permission of Hodder & Stoughton, a member of the Hodder Headline Group. All rights reserved. "NIV" is a trademark of International Bible Society. UK trademark number 1448790. Scripture quotations marked "NLT" are taken from the Holy Bible, New Living Translation, copyright © 1996, 2004, 2007 by Tyndale House Foundation. Used by permission of Tyndale House Publishers, Inc., Carol Stream, Illinois 60188. All rights reserved. The extract marked "AV" is from The Authorized (King James) Version. Rights in the Authorized Version are vested in the Crown. Reproduced by permission of the Crown's patentee, Cambridge University Press.
Extract on p. 69 taken from the song "Something Beautiful" by William J. Gaither/Gloria Gaither. Copyright © 1971 William J. Gaither, Inc. of Gaither Copyright Management Adm. in the UK by Kingswaysongs, a division of David C Cook tym@kingsway.co.uk Used by permission.

A catalogue record for this book is available from the British Library

Printed and bound in China, August 2022, LH54

Dedicated

to

Mum and Dad,

who always encouraged me to

"trace the rainbow through the rain"

Foreword

The Christian book market today is filled with thousands upon thousands of volumes. I have no idea how one chooses what should be read. Occasionally, very occasionally, one comes across a volume that in reality is a must for everybody.

Rainbows for Rainy Days is one such book. As I started reading it, I was immediately attracted by the story. It begins by talking about Noah and his rainbow. I am writing from Baghdad, and without doubt we know that Noah was here in Iraq. So that was my first attraction.

The other attraction at the very heart of this little book is the concept of living in a broken-hearted world. Yet in the midst of this pain and suffering, a pain that Catherine knows not least because of the death of her daughters, the glory of God shines through. I sit here in Baghdad surrounded by suffering. Of the thousands in my congregation I do not know one person who has not endured great anguish and the death of loved ones. This book takes you to the Holy Bible and there provides both solace and great hope.

One passage that truly caught my attention was where Catherine says: "So when you go to worship this Sunday, don't be overwhelmed by a congregation of thousands, or disappointed by a congregation of dozens. Instead, be captivated by the One who is 'in the midst'." The Lord of Glory in the midst uniquely fills these pages. This is a simply wonderful book. Enjoy!

Canon Andrew P. B. White
Anglican Chaplain to Iraq

Preface

I had noticed her before she reached me, her thin frame bent over with age and arthritic knuckles stretched white as she leaned heavily on the walking stick. Her face was still hidden from view as she measured the floor between us with her eyes. Then, as this very elderly lady came up level with me, she stopped, and her gaze finally met mine.

"I wanted to tell you how much your little book has meant to me," she said, a huge grin now adding to the landscape of her wrinkled face. Before I had time to reply she continued, "It sits beside my bed, and I have read a reading from it each night since it was given to me as a gift."

Deeply moved, I soon realized from our conversation that she must have read *Rainbows for Rainy Days* at least thirty-six times!

"I think you need to put a request for a new devotional on your Christmas list," I joked.

"Oh no, dear," she replied firmly. "Not until God stops blessing me through this one!"

It's humbling to think how a little book, which started its life as a small 6 x 4 devotional on the promises of God, could have blessed others in the way it has. That, I believe, has little to do with me and all to do with the God who cares deeply about the storms that hit our lives.

Back in 2008, when I wrote the first edition of *Rainbows for Rainy Days*, I was simply sharing what God had already spoken into my own life. By the time it was finished I would not have worried had no one ever bought the book. I had had the most inestimable pleasure of God's ministry to my own soul during the six weeks that it took to write. That in itself was reward enough.

And now I am further privileged to have been invited by Monarch to revise and expand the original into this second edition that you now hold in your hands.

Special thanks go to Liz Young, and to my husband, Philip, both of whom encouraged me with words of wisdom and correction. Also a big thank you to Tony Collins of Monarch, who is allowing *Rainbows for Rainy Days* to have a second life in such a lovely format.

Don't worry, I don't expect you to read it thirty-six times! But I do pray that as you "wait upon the Lord" you will glimpse God's rainbow in His promise to "renew your strength" (Isaiah 40:31).

Catherine Campbell

1

"I have set my rainbow in the clouds, and it will
be the sign of the covenant between me and the
earth… Never again will the waters become a flood
to destroy all life."

Genesis 9:13, 15 (NIV)

The excitement on board was tangible as the *Maid of the Mist*
headed for the American side of the great Niagara Falls. Gasps of
both sheer delight and trepidation came from the crowd as the little
boat seemed to reduce in size even further beside the magnitude
of the white water cascading over the steep rock face. We felt like
trespassers! Insignificant beside such grandeur.

The water beneath us was bubbling and swelling under
the sheer force of its rival above. And then we saw it – right in
the middle of all that turbulence, that persistent watery storm: a
rainbow!

Transported back to the time of Noah, I could hear God make
His covenant, not only with that great Patriarch of the faith, but
with all generations to follow. "I have set My rainbow in the cloud,"
said the Lord, as a reminder to Noah of His continued protection
and presence. Noah was just emerging from his "dark night of the

soul", having survived the devastation of the flood alone but for his family. Only the God who made him understood the fear that would overshadow his heart every time a cloud crossed the sky!

Only the God who made him loved him enough to put a visible sign of the promise of His divine presence into the very thing that frightened Noah most: the cloud!

And there, in that dramatically beautiful place, God was reminding me that He had a rainbow for *my* every cloud too. "I've set My rainbow in the cloud," I could hear Him say. "If you look deep into every storm of life, you will see Me there. That is My promise to you."

2

"For I consider that the sufferings of this present time are not worthy to be compared with the glory which shall be revealed in us."

Romans 8:18

It's such a little word. Only three letters long. Yet this word has broken hearts, divided families, separated friends, devastated lives, and destroyed faith. Intellectuals have puzzled over it, scientists have tried to explain it and philosophers have played mind games with it, while theologians have tried to spiritualize it… all to no avail.

I doubt if there is one person alive who has not used it, and few who have not tried to find a satisfactory answer to it. There just doesn't seem to be one.

Why? Why should millions starve? Why should children live with abuse? Why does evil prevail? Why should natural disasters wipe out those who already have so little? Why should my husband lose his job, or my child suffer pain? Why should my friend have cancer, or my father dementia? Why do Christians still face torture across our world? Why doesn't God do something to stop all this suffering?

This question can be answered in part by recognizing that we live in a fallen world, yet for the most part we just don't have an answer to the sufferings experienced by individuals or nations. The tragedy, however, is made worse when we allow what we don't know to rob us of what we do know.

In this verse the apostle Paul, a man who knew more than most about difficulty, encourages us to compare what we are going through now – our suffering – with what lies ahead for us: glory. Don't concentrate on your pain, is his message. Instead, think of Heaven ahead.

So hang on in there! Compared to our promised future, our present sufferings pale into insignificance. Hold on to what you know – glory is up ahead!

3

"… the sorrows of widowhood will be remembered no more, for your Creator will be your husband. The LORD Almighty is His name!"

Isaiah 54:4–5

There was a slight air of nervousness as the ladies arrived. Greetings were exchanged, the weather discussed, and the hostess's beautiful cross-stitch pictures provided a natural talking point. This was not the first time these ladies had met. But tonight would be different – and I felt totally out of my depth. I was unique in that room: the only woman present whose husband would be waiting for her when she got home. All the others had been widowed.

Some had been widowed for decades, and my heart broke for them as they revisited places long since locked away in the private recesses of their heart. Bravely each of them spoke of a beloved husband and the day of his death, offering help to those who had been a shorter time on that lonely road, yet savouring a rare opportunity to speak once again of the one who had once filled their life with love.

For others the wounds were still raw, as only a short time had passed since they had said their final farewell. In spite of this, the strategically placed box of tissues was barely used, as each drew strength from the others, realizing that the room was filled with those who *really* knew how they felt.

From the quiet corner of the sofa a gentle yet profound statement fell from the lips of a very private woman. "I have discovered," she said, as a warm smile crossed her face, "that I still have a husband." Stillness fell as she continued. "He sits with me in the morning, and He listens to all I say. He keeps me company when I walk to the shops, and assures me that He will be with me through the night when I reach for the bedside lamp."

Heaven visited that room as she concluded: "The Lord Almighty is His name."

4

"Then I realized that these pleasures are from the hand of God. For who can eat or enjoy anything apart from him?"

Ecclesiastes 2:24b–25 (NLT)

There is still a perception around today of God as a hard taskmaster: distant and without emotion towards His children. Even we who belong to Him may sometimes doubt His love, especially when times are tough.

The reality, however, couldn't be more different. Jesus taught  His disciples in Matthew 7:11 that our heavenly Father has a giving heart that far exceeds ours as earthly parents. And there are even times when He surprises us with tangible expressions of His fatherly love.

Philip's jaw dropped as he looked at the price list beside the entrance gate. It looked as though Plan B was going to fill his day rather than watching a football match from the top division at Selhurst Park. Tired after preaching at a busy week of meetings in a church near London, my husband was glad to have the Saturday off to relax. Coming from Northern Ireland, opportunities to see a "big game" were rare, so he had been excited at the prospect as he travelled into the city.

But now, with his hands pushed deep into his pockets, he let out a deep sigh of disappointment. It looked as if he would have to make do with a walk around the sights of London, the price of a ticket being far beyond what he could afford.

As he looked longingly at the prohibitive price list one more time, he felt a hand touch his shoulder.

"Do you want to go in?" the stranger asked.

Before Philip had time to reply, the stranger continued, his face creased with a friendly smile: "My wife and I are season ticket holders but she's not free today, so you're welcome to use her ticket… if you like?"

Stammering like a child, Philip thanked the man and followed him into the massive football ground. The man turned away from the normal entrance towards the one marked "PLAYERS and OFFICIALS", with Philip walking close behind, wide-eyed and speechless, unable to believe what was happening.

Moments later, they took their seats, right next to the Directors' Box! When the half-time whistle blew, the humble preacher was treated to tea and sandwiches in the Directors' Lounge!

It was a day he has never forgotten; not because of the football game but because he "realized that these pleasures were from the hand of God".

When did you last allow yourself to see God's hand in some little unexpected kindness? He is after all a Father who loves to give His children good things.

5

"Arise and eat, because the journey
is too great for you."

1 Kings 19:7

God never ceases to amaze me. These eleven words have humbled me, comforted me, given me hope, and caused my heart to soar. The God of Heaven knows when "the journey is too great" for me; when my body is too tired; when my mind loses the ability to function normally; when the dark clouds of despair blot out any reason to go on; when the loneliness of my situation consumes me.

And He not only knows – He acts in tenderness to enable me to continue the journey.

Elijah is the perfect example. He had definitely had enough. Having delivered God's message of judgement to Ahab, he was fed by ravens in the desert, cared for by a pagan widow in a foreign land; he returned to challenge the prophets of Baal on Mount Carmel, rebuked the backslidden people of Israel, rebuilt the altar, witnessed the miraculous – fire from Heaven and rain after drought – and then ran in front of Ahab's chariot all the way to Jezreel, some twenty miles. Phew!

Then what happens? The threats of a woman send him running in fear of his life, and the great prophet is found in the wilderness,

languishing under a juniper tree – exhausted, dejected, fearful and utterly depressed, pleading with God to take his life!

God's response? He sends a ministering angel. No wagging finger, no lectures, no tutting, and no accusations of failure. Instead God utters some of the tenderest words in Scripture to this broken servant. "I know the journey is too great for you," He whispers – and follows that with breakfast! And by those acts of compassion Elijah is enabled to move on once more.

Remember, our cries of despair are *always* heard in Heaven – and are responded to by a compassionate Father who knows and acts on our behalf. So be on the lookout for ministering angels – they really do exist!

6

"Trust in the LORD with all your heart, and lean not on your own understanding. In all your ways acknowledge Him, and He shall direct your paths."

Proverbs 3:5–6

My mother-in-law exercised the wonderful gift of encouragement through the dying art of letter-writing. For many decades her beautiful handwritten epistles traversed the world to bless the lives of missionaries. By van, train, plane or boat her love and prayerful concern reached God's servants in both cities of millions and small jungle villages alike. Ignoring the age of electronic communication she painstakingly kept putting pen to paper, and touched the lives of more people than we will ever know.

If you ever received a birthday card from her, it was never only once, but faithfully, year after year. Annie never forgot.

As one of those on her very long birthday card list, I was a grateful recipient, yet at times her postscripts made me chuckle. You see, she always used the same Bible verse to end each birthday greeting: Proverbs 3:5–6. Every year there it was… just like the previous year!

Privately I would smile and I was even bold enough to question: "Does she not know any other Bible verses?"

Shortly after her death, I affectionately turned to Proverbs 3:5–6 to examine the verses that she had constantly passed on to others. As I read them I discovered not only the wisdom given by God to Solomon, but also the heart of a woman who loved God.

"Trust in the Lord with all your heart…" Half-hearted trust is no trust at all. *Give God your all*, was Annie's advice to those she loved.

"Lean not on your own understanding…" *What little we know will never take us through the hard times*, her postscript whispered in my ear.

Her voice was stronger in my head now. "In all your ways acknowledge Him…" *Make sure He's the One who gets the credit for everything in your life.*

And then I could see that she wanted me to read this amazing promise… year after year after year: "And He shall direct your paths." I could almost hear her say, *Catherine, when He has your all, and you trust Him with what you don't understand, thanking Him for everything in your life, then, wonder of all wonders, He will be your guide… even down the darkest of paths.*

As I closed my Bible, I smiled again, recognizing that there was no foolishness in Annie's annual postscripts… only godly wisdom.

7

"The LORD is my shepherd; I shall not want."

Psalm 23:1

Some experiences in life always remain with you – like my first journey on the mountain railway in the Bernese Oberland of Switzerland.

As the train pulled out of the small station our host enthused over the engineering feats that had been accomplished to enable this quaint vehicle to climb along the sides of mountains at steep gradients. I tried to conceal my nervousness, hiding my terror of heights, and convincing myself that she was surely exaggerating. Soon the sheer beauty of our surroundings calmed and enthralled me, as the train passed through lush rolling valleys, and alongside azure blue lakes. In the distance, mountain peaks draped in eternal snow played hide and seek among the wispy clouds, while defying the reality of the blistering heat in the valleys below.

The picture-postcard Swiss chalets were built in the most unlikely of places, and added new meaning to the phrase "room with a view". However, our host chuckled when I questioned her on why garden sheds had been built up in the mountains.

"They are shepherds' huts," she replied. "Once the snow melts from the lower foothills, usually around May, the sheep are brought back onto the mountain for summer grazing." She went on to explain how the shepherd stays with the flock, moving from pasture to pasture, protecting and caring for his sheep. Then once a week, family or friends would bring fresh food and clothes, and leave them in the tiny wooden huts that dot the mountainside. Only when the weather changes at the end of September does the shepherd see home again. "To be a shepherd requires sacrifice," she added.

As I mused on what I had just heard, I thought of the psalmist, who knew exactly what life was like for these shepherds, centuries later. The psalmist David was the shepherd who became a king, yet Jesus was the King of all kings who became *the* Shepherd.

The sacrifice of the Great Shepherd for us, His sheep, involved more than leaving home (although He did that), more than distancing Himself from His Father (although He did that as well), and more than putting Himself in danger in a hostile environment (which He did willingly). His sacrifice for us was complete, for He laid down His life for His sheep (John 10:15).

Now why did He do that? Verse 1 of Psalm 23 gives us the answer: in order that "I shall not want". My Shepherd has promised to provide "all that I need" (NLT), so why should I be afraid?

8

"When you pass through the waters, I will be with you; And through the rivers, they shall not overflow you… for I am the LORD your God."

Isaiah 43:2–3

I don't know what it is about a newborn baby that captures your heart so completely. Perhaps it is the sight of perfection in miniature: the tiny toes and fingers; the wrinkled skin that almost looks too big for such a small frame, while feeling softer than the exquisite work of the rarest silkworm. Or maybe it is the unrepeatable expressions that cross her beautiful face as she sleeps, the smell of baby powder, the feeling of utter dependence on you for her every need. I just do not know. I only know that our firstborn stole my heart, as well as that of her proud daddy. This beautiful, blue-eyed blonde wrapped her little life around our hearts tighter with every passing day.

Then, barely seven months later, the words of a paediatrician swept through our lives like a tornado, wreaking havoc and turning our hitherto ordered lives upside down. His words destroyed our plans, devastated our family, clouded our future… and broke our hearts. "Mrs Campbell," he said, "don't you realize that your little girl is handicapped – she will never be normal!"

The anguish of soul that followed this diagnosis threw my life into a very dark place of pain, confusion, disbelief, and despair.

The tragedies of life have a way of doing that, don't they? One minute life is wonderful, and the next, everything is falling apart. Your safety and security are all gone in an instant. Your relationship with God is dented, because you cannot understand how He could possibly allow such a thing to happen to you – His child.

Yet the words of Isaiah 43 minister clearly to us in two distinct ways. The word "when" assures us that our difficulty is not a personal attack. Rather, it is a common occurrence in a fallen world from which Christians aren't exempt. But even more comforting is that the God who has called us by name (Isaiah 43:1) has promised us that He will walk with us through every storm that batters our lives.

Imagine – never alone! Instead, always accompanied… by the One who is bigger than anything life can throw at us!

9

"And you will seek Me and find Me, when you search for Me with all your heart."

Jeremiah 29:13

"A man's word is his bond", declares the old saying. Yet in today's world I have doubts that those words still stand true. Tradesmen rarely turn up on time, politicians do not make good on pre-election promises, guarantees usually have get-out clauses… Even friends let you down at times: phone calls don't happen and visits are cancelled too easily. And that is only what others do to us! What about our "word"? Can we be trusted to do as we say?

Thankfully God is not like us. Paul tells us in his letter to Titus (1:2) that "God… cannot lie". He always keeps His word. In fact it is even better than that. He keeps His word even if we do not know what it says!

When I was just fourteen years old I did not know what the verse printed at the top of this page said – but God did. And God knew that I was desperately seeking to know what it meant to be a real Christian. Humanly speaking I was doing everything right. I went to church every Sunday, read my Bible, didn't do anyone any harm – surely that was all that was needed to make me a Christian? But it wasn't. Then, when I came across real Christians for the first

time, I cried out to God to show me what it meant to be a "real" Christian. And God remembered what He had said in Jeremiah 29:13, and He saw a teenager search for Him with all her heart. And because He keeps His word, I found Him.

Recognizing my sin, and repenting of it in light of the sacrifice of Jesus on the cross, was all it took to make me one of God's children. That and the unswerving reality that God can be trusted, because He *always* keeps His word – even when we are unaware of what His word says.

Perhaps as you read this you are still seeking, unsure of your own relationship with God. Take heart, for if you seek Him, and search for Him with *all* your heart, you *will* find Him. He has already promised.

10

"Teacher, do You not care that we are perishing?"

Mark 4:38b

Disappointment often bruises, disturbing our peace, with the potential to wound us deeply; especially if the source of our disappointment involves someone we love and trust. Broken promises, deceitful actions, lies, and abandonment... these are the building blocks of disappointment.

Unfortunately, each of us has probably been both the cause and the one to experience disappointment at some time or other. When laced with an "I don't care" attitude, it also becomes destructive. However, it is equally dangerous to treat our perceptions as fact: merely believing that someone doesn't care doesn't make it true. Take the disciples in this story in Mark 4:35–41, for instance.

They had just had the most amazing time with Jesus. Coming down the mountain with the words of the Sermon on the Mount still ringing in their ears, they went on to witness many miracles. A man with leprosy was healed by Jesus' touch. A centurion's servant was made well from a distance by Jesus' words. Peter's own mother-in-law was restored to health so completely that she immediately got up and cooked them a meal!

Yet when the disciples were in a boat a short time later and a storm whipped up around them, panic set in. They were terrified. This wasn't supposed to happen. After all, Jesus was in the boat! And in their fear and disappointment they jumped to the wrong conclusion: Jesus didn't care about them! He was actually sleeping in the back of the boat. If He cared for them He wouldn't let this happen to them… would He?

Accosting Jesus with the words: "Teacher, do You not care that we are perishing?" the disciples failed to recognize that Jesus was not asleep because He didn't care, but because *the storm neither surprised nor concerned Him.* Jesus already knew what the disciples would discover soon enough: that "even the wind and the sea obey Him" (Mark 4:41). Their emotional calculation was flawed, and they got it so wrong! At times, I too have added two and two together and come up with something other than four. How often I have struggled with disappointment. "Surely God wouldn't let this happen to me?" I have grumbled. "I am His child after all!" Thankfully, God is a willing and kind teacher, as He has reminded me more than once that Jesus' presence in the boat doesn't necessarily stop the storm from coming.

Rather, His presence ensures that my boat does not sink!

And as I take my eye off the storm and fix it instead on the Storm-Stiller, I discover that He's been in control the whole time.

For "even the wind and the sea obey Him".

11

"For where two or three are gathered together in My name, I am there in the midst of them."

Matthew 18:20

I couldn't help but smile as the taxi made its way down the driveway to the set-down area in front of the large church building. Only in America could the parking bays be named after the fruit of the Spirit! (I wondered if those parked in "Patience" were the last to leave every Sunday morning!)

I am ashamed to say it, but I was rather sceptical when we took our seats in the huge auditorium. I was prejudging – expecting the service in this mega-church to be over the top in every way. More "show" than church as I knew it.

It certainly was not church as I knew it, but it took no time at all for the sense of God's presence first to

convict me and then to bless and challenge my soul. I worshipped the God of Heaven that morning with thousands of others, and was held spellbound by testimonies of grace and the preaching of God's precious word. Without a doubt the Lord was "in the midst".

The following Sunday we attended a little white clapboard building in a not-so-salubrious area of town. There was no driveway and no parking lot. Only a few dozen people were at the service, yet as visitors we were welcomed like royalty. At the appropriate time most of the congregation emptied into the choir stalls for their "anthem". The singing was awful, yet it brought tears to my eyes and undoubtedly delight in Heaven, for these people loved their Saviour.

The pastor preached a simple, direct sermon – so direct, in fact, that he called out people's names as he spoke the word of God into their hearts and situations. It was obvious that he knew his "flock" well, and had seen many of them through hard times. And my heart was overwhelmed as I worshipped with these people, because the Lord was "in the midst".

So when you go to worship this Sunday, don't be overwhelmed by a congregation of thousands, or disappointed by a congregation of dozens. Instead, be captivated by the One who is "in the midst".

12

"… and every branch that bears fruit He prunes,
that it may bear more fruit."

John 15:2

I hate gardening! My parents, on the other hand, tend their garden with care, and I always enjoy inspecting any new additions that have been planted since my last visit. On one occasion a shocking sight met me as I made my way to the front door. The beautiful yellow rose bush we had bought them for an anniversary gift had all but disappeared, except for a measly little stump protruding from the ground.

Just a short time before, this very bush had been resplendent in full colourful bloom. Now it looked naked and damaged – never to be the same again as far as I was concerned.

"What happened to your beautiful rose bush?" were the words that met my mother as she opened the door.

"Oh, I just pruned it back," she replied nonchalantly. "It was so beautiful this year that I thought a good pruning would guarantee an even better show next summer."

"I think you have overdone it this time, Mum," was my critical response.

"Just you wait and see," she smiled, as we went inside.

As usual she was right, for the following year the bush was displaying huge, fragrant blooms… all helped along by the pruning!

In John 15 we read of the "Vine Life", and how we have been grafted into the true Vine (Christ) by the divine Gardener (the Father). We learn that abiding in the Vine is essential if we are to bear the type of fruit that identifies us as authentic branches: the fruit of the Spirit, that is – as described in Galatians 5:22–23.

But this type of "fruit" is only produced by pruning. It is easy to understand how spiritual "suckers" or dead leaves should be removed to encourage a healthy plant – often laziness and disobedience, for example, mar our effectiveness – but the more radical work of the divine Gardener can bring shock and questioning. It is difficult to understand why that part of our lives that seems good needs to be touched at all, and painful pruning leaves us feeling naked and damaged… perhaps even to the point of wondering if we will ever be the same again.

Yet this verse promises us that in the days to come, the barren, ugly sight of pruning will be replaced by something beautiful. This in turn will cause us to bear even more fruit than previously, as the strength of the true Vine is enabled to flow through us.

And remember – watering and weeding can be done from a distance, but the Gardener has to be close to the vine when He is pruning it!

13

"… be sure your sin will find you out."

Numbers 32:23

Not exactly a cheery thought to greet your day, is it? This is the kind of verse that makes me think of doom and gloom merchants – placard-carrying, finger-waving, solemn-faced individuals who love to speak of judgement and forget about grace.

How wrong we can be. This is after all a promise of Scripture – our sin will be found out. But it was only during a study on the life of Bathsheba, in 2 Samuel 11 onwards, that I discovered that this verse is as much about *mercy* as it is about judgement.

The story of Bathsheba's adulterous relationship with King David is a sordid affair, resulting in the "murder" of her husband and the death of her infant son. Somehow, both she and David had forgotten what the Law said. Sin cannot be hidden. The sad story unfolds of a woman who is tested by sin and tried by suffering, and yet she comes through triumphant – and it is due in greater part to this verse.

You see, if Bathsheba's sin had not "found her out", she might never have sought the mercy and forgiveness of God. The clues of her repentance are revealed for us in 2 Samuel 12. When her second son was born she named him Solomon, meaning "Peaceful". Only

a woman at peace with God could be free to use such a name. And we also read that God named this child as well – Jedidiah, meaning "Beloved of the Lord" – showing this repentant woman that she had not merely been found out, but had also been shown the loving mercy of God.

Whether we have sinned in thought, word or deed makes no difference. There are no little sins or big sins in the eyes of a holy God – only the promise that one day our sin will find us out. Yet these words should be treated as good news, because they demonstrate to us just how much God loves us.

Numbers 32:23 is *not* a picture of an accusing God, but rather one of a *merciful* Father, who is giving us the opportunity to repent of our sin and accept His forgiveness. In God's book failure doesn't have to be final. So rejoice or repent – whichever your need is today!

14

> "And whatever you ask in My name, that I will do, that the Father may be glorified in the Son. If you ask anything in My name, I will do it."

> John 14:13–14

This promise, spoken by Jesus to His disciples, is truly powerful. Yet the practical reality of living in it is particularly difficult for those of us struggling with the question of unanswered prayer. Long periods of time often pass while we sit in God's waiting room, and the result may be a loss of confidence in our prayer lives.

I know that feeling only too well, hence my reluctance to include this promise in a book that is meant to offer encouragement. But God said: "Put it in, Catherine. There are lots of people who struggle just like you."

It is heartbreaking to sit with someone who is suffering and they look you in the eye and say: "I've prayed and prayed. Why doesn't God take this pain away?" And you simply can't answer, because you don't know why God is silent on this occasion.

Unfortunately, one of the negative impacts of Heaven's perceived silence can be that we stop praying the big prayers altogether. We keep to the safe and the repetitive – "God bless so and so" – and avoid the specific, direct requests that Jesus is urging

His disciples to pray in the context of these verses.

Staying "safe" has been a problem with my prayer life that I have frequently had to revisit. Thankfully God is a patient teacher and loving Father!

Running parallel to that is the way in which we bring our prayer requests to God. I have discovered from both praying and listening that we have a tendency to pray answers rather than requests. Our prayer package has more to do with telling God what needs to be done and how He should do it. Therefore when God answers in a way that we don't want or expect, we find it difficult to accept.

There have been times when I haven't got things my way, only to discover later that God's way was much better. In short it was a good job He didn't do what I told Him to do!

I read these verses once during one of my prayer "struggling" times. As I mulled over the words in the context of the passage I was almost trying to find some evidence that this promise was exclusively for those Jesus was speaking to at that time. The response came in the form of God's quiet voice whispering to my heart: "You are missing so much by not praying the big prayers, Catherine. There is so much I want to teach you, yet you stand on the sidelines."

"I'm afraid, Lord. My track record hasn't been too good so far."

"I only want you to pray the prayers, Catherine. The answers are My responsibility!"

And I wondered how much I had missed of God's blessing and power along the way, and if Heaven has been silent because God is waiting to hear me ask in faith.

This is a promise we should grasp with both hands and we can start it with a big prayer: "Lord, teach us to pray" (Luke 11:1).

15

> "And God is faithful; he will not let you be tempted beyond what you can bear."
>
> 1 Corinthians 10:13 (NIV)

Both of our daughters had multiple disabilities, requiring everything to be done for them, so for a period of almost twenty years my husband and I rarely knew what it was to have a good night's sleep.

We had a workable system, though, whereby he stayed up, whenever needed, for the earlier part of the night, while I managed the hours after 1 a.m. I found that I couldn't function once exhaustion had set in, as it usually did, around 10 p.m.; but after a few hours' sleep I was capable of getting up and down numerous times a night.

The problems arose when Philip's ministry as an evangelist took him away from home, and I had to cover the whole night single-handed.

Sleep deprivation is a dreadful experience; physical exhaustion allows the floodgates of emotional distress to be thrown open and coping strategies to flounder.

A busy day had rolled into a sleepless night, and although Cheryl drifted off once she had been turned over, Joy was showing no sign of settling. She was fretful and nothing I did seemed to work. I tried every trick in the book, but the more exhausted I became the more she cried. I sang to her, rocked her, changed her, and prayed with her, but she still wouldn't stop crying.

Eventually her cheeks were as wet with my tears as they were with her own, and I propped her up in bed and sank to my knees. "You promised me, God," I cried out. "You promised that… that… I wouldn't be tempted beyond what I could bear. Well, I can't take any more, God – I just can't take any more!" My sobbing silenced my pleas as I buried my head in Joy's duvet.

Before I realized what had happened I opened my eyes. I had been asleep for I don't know how long. And then I noticed it: the silence. It was beautiful. Joy was fast asleep – peacefully so, in fact. And my heart felt strangely quiet – distress and anxiety wiped away. "You heard me, Lord," I whispered, as I slid into my own bed.

That was when I realized how foolish my comments were. God didn't need to be reminded of His promise. He is not some kind of forgetful old man who needs a bit of a prodding now and again. In His mercy God is constantly keeping promises we are not even aware of, but He does expect us to trust Him with the ones we already know.

He really does know when we have reached our limit. Repeating the promise is for *our* benefit, not His.

16

"You keep track of all my sorrows. You have collected all my tears in your bottle. You have recorded each one in your book."

Psalm 56:8 (NLT)

Tears cause a conundrum for Christians. We all have them, but we don't like them. Somehow they seem to represent weakness at best or a lack of spirituality at worst. We torture ourselves with the concept that people with *real* faith unquestioningly trust God in every situation. Therefore we allow no room for tears, and definitely not in public!

That is how I used to think, so when our ten-year-old daughter died a mere two weeks before Christmas I accepted my initial sorrow, but as time passed I constantly reprimanded myself for crying. However, I seemed totally unable to rectify the situation. There were no "dry" days in my life. I cried every day, and then I asked God to forgive me for crying, feeling somehow that I was letting Him down.

There were even times when I actually hid from those who called at my home, not wanting them to see the state I was in. On one such occasion the doorbell rang and I secreted myself away in the kitchen, praying that they would go away. But this visitor was not so easily put off. To my horror I saw a shadow pass the window and head for the back door. Like a fool I pulled a towel over my head, imagining that if I couldn't see them they wouldn't see me.

I heard the back door open and a familiar voice speak my name. "Catherine, what are you doing, love?" questioned my confused mother. As she made her way towards me I fell into her arms.

"I can't stop crying, Mum," I replied, rebuking myself as she held me the way that only a mother can. "I shouldn't be like this… I should be stronger!"

She let me cry myself out and then gently whispered in my ear: "It's okay to cry, love," as she rubbed my back. "In fact, God thinks so much of your tears that He collects them in a bottle!"

I pulled back in amazement. "He does what?" I exclaimed.

"Psalm 56 says that He collects our tears in a bottle," she replied.

And I started to laugh. "Just imagine, Mum. There must be *crates* up there with my name on them!" My eyes may have been puffy and my head sore, but my heart was lightened by the thought of a God who is "touched with the feeling of our infirmities" (Hebrews 4:15, AV) to such an extent that He counts our tears as precious.

And so ends the conundrum. The God who created us with the ability to shed tears not only gives us permission to use them without guilt, He even keeps track of all the sorrows that cause them!

17

"But those who wait on the LORD shall renew their strength; they shall mount up with wings like eagles, they shall run and not be weary, they shall walk and not faint."

Isaiah 40:31

Many of the promises of God are conditional. The God who made us is relational in nature – He wants to work with us, and therefore some promises require our input if they are to be fulfilled.

In this verse we are promised renewed strength, energy instead of weariness, and an ability to carry on in the mundane daily round. If we are honest, which of us wouldn't like all three? Yet how often have we woken in the morning knowing that the problem, or the pain, or the unpaid bill has not disappeared with the sleep of the receding night? And we wonder how we will get through another day.

Our response seems so logical, so natural. We worry and fret ourselves into exhaustion, allowing a weariness of soul to engulf us. Yet God *has* promised us strength and energy and endurance… IF we "wait on the LORD". Why do we find that so hard? I believe it all boils down to one thing: a question of trust.

The great eagle cannot reach the heights that it does merely by its own strength. As it spreads its strong, impressive wings the bird allows the wind to carry it to places no other bird can go: above the perilous cliffs, beyond the dangers of other creatures, to skies where it can see for miles below. This kind of flying appears effortless because the eagle is trusting in a power bigger than itself: the wind.

God wants to take *us* to places above our problems. He wants to help us see beyond ourselves to His bigger picture. He longs to empower us and energize us for the little niggles of life, as well as the personal tsunamis that seek to destroy us. But in this case He requires our co-operation. We need to "wait on the LORD".

It is time to stop flapping around and trying to muster the strength to survive on our own. It will require stillness. It will require trust. It will require us to stop… wait… and set our spiritual "wings" for the supernatural power of God to lift us beyond the now.

Then we simply watch, for the rest is up to God.

18

"For thus says the LORD God of Israel: 'The bin of flour shall not be used up, nor shall the jar of oil run dry, until the day the LORD sends rain on the earth.'"

1 Kings 17:14

This is a beautiful story of God's provision for two completely different individuals. First, it tells how Elijah experiences the truth of God's ability to care for him outside his personal comfort zone. He has been told to leave Israel and go to a foreign land (actually to the hometown of his arch enemy, Jezebel). Once there he is to accept the hospitality of a pagan widow – and a starving one at that! Doesn't sound too promising, does it?

Then we read about God's promise to this woman, through the words of His prophet: "Make me a small cake from it first... and afterward make some for yourself and your son" (verse 13). This seemingly selfish request is quickly followed by the amazing promise printed above. What should she do? Up to now she has merely heard of the God of Israel. Can she trust the words of His prophet? Can He really do this miraculous thing for her and her son?

Both situations required obedience and faith in order that God's provision would be granted. Both individuals were in dire straits, and probably neither was comfortable with what was being asked of them – yet they both responded in ways that ultimately saved and changed their lives.

There is no doubt that this verse was a specific promise for a specific individual, but echoed in this story we also see the principles of God's provision for us in hard times.

On occasion God takes us out of our comfort zone in order that we can experience the truth of what Paul said to the Philippian church: "My God shall supply all your need according to His riches in glory by Christ Jesus" (Philippians 4:19). Both Old and New Testament confirm that at times of financial distress, or when we are physically unable to meet our own needs, God can provide aid for us in a supernatural way.

I am not speaking here of "prosperity gospel" nonsense, but rather of the action of a loving heavenly Father who knows every situation of our lives, including our work, our finances, and the needs of our families.

At the time of writing, much of the world is experiencing the "credit crunch". Prices are rising, incomes are falling, and jobs are going. Yet I firmly believe that the God who looked after a prophet by the hands of a starving widow in the middle of a drought can look after you and me too.

19

"For nothing is impossible with God."

Luke 1:37 (NLT)

When I am writing I sometimes need to find a name for one of my characters, and I have often found "Professor Google" very helpful.

In the West we tend to name our children after a relative or – perish the thought – after a celebrity! You only have to examine a school roll to discover what's currently trendy as far as boys' and girls' names are concerned. However, in the East the old tradition of using names that have a significant meaning is still widely practised today.

In the Bible names are very significant. Even the names God uses for Himself, and the timing of their introduction is of importance.

Take the name El-Shaddai, for example.

It was first used in the Old Testament when God confirmed His promise to Abraham that Sarah was going to have a baby in her old age (Genesis 17:1). Historically the name has been used in conjunction with statements of covenant promise. God was making a promise involving the continuation of the covenantal line, and so He referred to Himself as El-Shaddai.

In simple terms El-Shaddai means "Almighty God". If you peel back another layer in its Hebraic meaning, linguistic scholars have translated it as "God who is sufficient" or simply "God who is enough".

Imagine God's perfect timing in revealing Himself as "God who is enough" to Abraham for the very first time. Abraham was staring the impossible in the face: "'How could I become a father at the age of 100?' he thought. 'And how can Sarah have a baby when she is ninety years old?'" (Genesis 17:17, NLT).

And God declared Himself as El-Shaddai – "God who is enough" – in the face of Abraham's mocking doubt. And the covenant-keeping God came through, making possible the impossible, when Sarah gave birth to Isaac.

Centuries later, a young teenage virgin also faced the impossible when she had an angelic visitation declaring that she would have a child. "And you are to give him the name Jesus," she was told in Luke's Gospel (1:31, NIV). Nine months later that same virgin held in her arms the long-awaited Messiah, the Son of God.

Mary learned, like Abraham before her, that God is El-Shaddai – "God who is enough". And therefore nothing is impossible with God.

There are times in our lives when we face the impossible, the immovable, the unchangeable. It is at those times that I like to whisper His name, El-Shaddai.

For He is enough…

… when we are weary

… when we are weak

… when we have reached the end of ourselves.

That name has stretched all the way from Genesis to the cross, where we find He is enough for our sin, our salvation, and our eternal destiny.

20

> "'… For I know the plans I have for you,' says the LORD. 'They are plans for good and not for disaster, to give you a future and a hope.'"
>
> Jeremiah 29:11 (NLT)

I read this verse today in the daily reading plan I am using for this year. I couldn't help but smile as the words washed over my heart, and I thought how tender-hearted God is to remind me of this verse, on this day.

Today is our elder daughter's birthday. In fact it was her little sister's birthday just five days ago, and the memories of all the birthday fun we used to have as a family are simply delightful.

But Cheryl had only ten birthdays, and Joy had thirteen.

Both of our girls were born with a genetic condition that caused profound multiple disabilities, resulting in frail, sickly bodies. To many people their lives were a tragedy, and their existence futile. They couldn't walk or talk, or even hold their own heads up. I never heard them call my name, or felt them plant a kiss on my cheek.

Yet this was the verse that God whispered in my ear, very early one morning, as I was on my way to the hospital, ready to face what, to me, was one more disaster. Like Pilgrim of old, I felt a great weight on my shoulders – not of sin, but of sadness.

And then God said: "Catherine, I know the plans I have for you. They are for your good and not to harm you – no matter what it feels like. Hang on in there, My child. I do have a future and a hope for you… and for those you love."

We live in a world where health, wealth, and personal happiness are the hallmarks of success; where the opinion of others determines our worth. Value is based on outward appearance; little worth is attributed to those who do not fit the "norm".

If you happen to add disability or suffering to the mix, then your life hits the "disaster zone" as far as some are concerned. Perhaps even you feel that words like "good", "future", and "hope" aren't for you.

Don't listen to such lies! God is still your Creator… even if your legs don't work. God is still your loving Father… even if cancer is destroying your human frame. Take courage – He has plans for you that this world knows nothing about. And His plans for you are "not for disaster", but for your good. And what's more, they are the *only* plans that can give you "a future and a hope" greater than anything you could imagine.

So hang on in there, and keep looking up!

21

"I am the light of the world. He who follows
Me shall not walk in darkness, but have the
light of life."

John 8:12

I don't know about you, but when I hear thunder rumbling in the
distance I always make sure I check the torches in the house, and
leave a few candles in strategic places, just in case the lights go out!
Darkness can affect us in a number of ways.

If sudden, it can shock us and take us by surprise, leaving us
feeling vulnerable.

It can disorientate us, making us unsure of ourselves.

It can cause fear, even when others are present.

Familiar things can look different in the darkness, making us
doubt them.

The uncertainty of physical darkness may cause some to stay
indoors at night, while other types of darkness also affect our lives.
There is emotional darkness – those times when we feel a black cloud
constantly lurking above us; the darkness of illness and suffering;

the darkness of depression; the darkness of disappointment or unemployment… and the dreadful darkness of grief, when you wonder if the sun will ever shine again.

The Bible also speaks of another kind of darkness that is even more devastating than any of the above: spiritual darkness. This darkness is a refusal to walk in the light of God, and symbolizes ignorance, error, and sin (1 John 1:5–10).

But the one thing darkness ultimately makes us do is search for the Light.

By contrast light:

shows us where we are, and makes
    the way ahead clear;

dispels the darkness;

quietens our fears;

restores our confidence;

brings security and peace once more.

Just four chapters further on in the Gospel of John, Jesus reinforces the fact that as the Light of the World He can dispel the darkness that threatens our present life and eternal destiny. "All who put their trust in Me," Jesus says, "will no longer remain in the dark" (John 12:46, NLT).

Darkness cannot live where light is, so run to Jesus, the Light of the World, and watch the amazing change that takes place when you do!

22

"When the LORD saw that He had caught Moses'
attention, God called to him from the bush, 'Moses!
Moses!'"

Exodus 3:4

It took something really extraordinary for God to get Moses'
attention. In fact, God had to set a bush alight to divert Moses from
what he was doing so that he could listen to Him. Nothing unusual
about a burning bush in a desert, you might think. The incredible
heat of the Eastern sun often started fires. But this was different: the
bush wasn't destroyed by the fire.

So Moses stopped what he was doing to look, and while God
had his attention He surprised this one-time Egyptian prince by
calling him by name.

Moses' own feeble attempt at helping the children of Israel
had failed miserably when he had to run for his life into the desert.
Forty years had passed and Moses had contented himself with the
life of a shepherd. And although finding pasture for his flock meant
much time alone, even in the foothills of Horeb, the mountain of
God, Moses had not been listening for the voice of God.

Instead, God had to use something remarkable to get this
man's attention. Moses had to be turned aside from the "everyday"

to take time to listen to what God had to speak into his life.

For some of us, God will have to use the extraordinary to divert our attention from the "everyday" in order that He might speak into our lives. But when He does He always calls us by name; an indication of His tenderness as He unfolds what may be a difficult plan for us.

Just as burning bushes are not uncommon in the desert, so suffering is not uncommon in this world, which has been cursed by the Fall. And God may use sickness, failure, money difficulties, or even the death of a friend or loved one to stop us in our tracks. The method He uses is the channel through which His voice can be heard – if we are prepared to step aside and listen.

For Moses, this encounter with God involved questioning, heartache, and a long hard road ahead. The results would be a long time in coming, but God was inviting Moses to become part of His big plan: the rescue of His people, the Israelites, resulting ultimately in the coming of the Messiah.

For us, it may be just as difficult, and God may not lay out His plan as clearly as He did for Moses. But as the years have passed since God diverted my attention by the birth of our first handicapped daughter, I have discovered in some small way that we are part of His bigger plan for a lost humankind.

I find Paul's words in Philippians 1:12 written on my heart: "The things which happened to me have actually turned out for the furtherance of the gospel."

Remember that "burning bushes" are not for destruction but for instruction. And if God gets our attention, He always has something life-changing to say.

23

"I shall go to him, but he shall not return to me."

2 Samuel 12:23

A young woman approached me after a meeting where I was speaking on the topic of how to make sense out of suffering. I was totally unprepared for what she was about to tell me, and

for a fleeting moment I groaned inwardly, wondering at the relevance of what I had just said in light of her painful circumstances.

After releasing me from a tender hug, she gathered herself together and said: "We buried our first little baby seven weeks ago – she was only six weeks old – and I wanted to tell you how much strength and courage you have given me tonight." My heart melted as I empathized with her in her loss; I felt that her bravery was immense in one so young. In the moments that followed, we turned to this story of the death of David and Bathsheba's baby, and the beautiful promise it contains.

Scripture is strangely silent on the death of a baby, or the very young… except for this verse. David had pleaded with God for the child to be allowed to live, and yet in the end that was not to be. Humanly speaking his death seemed unfair, as with the death of all innocents, but the resulting words have shouted comfort down through the centuries to broken-hearted mothers and fathers.

"I shall go to him," David said, giving us proof that the child (and our child too!) was alive – in his eternal home: Heaven – while also assuring us that one day we will be together again. The reality that "he shall not return to me" is hard to bear, but is softened by the promise of eternal reunion.

As the young woman got up to go she said: "Aren't God's promises so wonderful?!"

I couldn't argue with that!

24

"My Presence will go with you, and I will give you rest… for you have found grace in My sight, and I know you by name."

Exodus 33:14, 17b

Have you ever felt invisible? Do you imagine that if you disappeared from the face of the earth no one would notice? Sometimes you look at others and you wish you could be like them; they ooze popularity. Anybody who is anybody knows them. Conversely, no one ever seems to remember *your* name!

All of us can feel insignificant at times. Yes, believe it or not, even those who appear to have it all together.

When I was a teenager I was known as Billy Fraser's sister. Then when I got married I was known as Philip Campbell's wife. Now there is nothing wrong with either of those descriptions, except that just sometimes I wish people had remembered *my* name!

Latterly I was turned down by two publishers, not because they didn't like my writing, but because no one knew my name – and it is *names* that sell books!

Rejection and poor self-image can result in misery and all kinds of personal problems. In a bid to redress the balance, the shelves of libraries and bookstores are coming down with a multitude of self-help resources. Courses that aim to build your confidence abound, while self-assertiveness training is the in thing.

And yet I wonder if you can really feel better inside by becoming the kind of person who made you feel insignificant in the first place. The desire to be recognized, or even to fit in, appears endemic in today's society, but neither brings lasting satisfaction.

What is overwhelmingly more important, however, is that God knows your name. You do not need to struggle or push yourself forward to gain recognition in Heaven. You are already known to the God who created you, and also to the One who gave His life for you on Calvary.

Jesus affirms in John 10:3 what God had said to Moses years earlier: "He calls his own sheep *by name* and leads them out" (my italics). And His promise to us is amazing: He guides us, goes with us, and gives us rest in a frenetic society where people feel the need to be noticed.

I can name-drop with the best of them. In fact I can't be bettered, as my name is mentioned in the courts of Heaven… and so is yours!

25

"I press toward the goal for the prize of the upward call of God in Christ Jesus."

Philippians 3:14

There was a buzz on the coach as we took our seats; the excitement tangible as the big tour of our holiday was about to begin.

Travelling through lush valleys, our anticipation was heightened as the coach driver informed us of what lay ahead on this visit to Grossglockner. We would be negotiating no fewer than thirty-five hairpin bends along the route that would take us to the summit of Austria's highest mountain, some 12,460 feet above sea level.

However, the first tinge of disappointment came with the sweep of the big windscreen wiper in front of the driver, clouds quickly darkening the sky. Soon rain, mist, and even snow obscured the upward view of the magnificent mountain we had come to see. Slow, tedious progress was made around treacherous bend after treacherous bend, poor visibility now causing a hint of nervousness to replace the excitement of what was billed as one of the most spectacular road journeys in Europe.

At times a sullen quietness filled the coach. We had come all this way and couldn't see a thing! But we pressed on, buoyed by the promise that the now-tedious journey would be worth it all.

"Just wait till the clouds clear," the driver said. "I promise you'll be glad you came." I had to admire his optimism.

By the time we arrived at the summit the rain had stopped, and buttoning up against the freezing wind, Philip and I headed away from the crowd in the direction of the eternal glacier.

As we walked, the sun came out, peeking through the clouds and eventually chasing away the blackness overhead. Marmots emerged from underground burrows, warming their thick brown fur in the sunshine. Alpine flowers swayed resplendent in the brisk wind, declaring their fortitude among the craggy rocks. And the glimpse of an eagle overhead took our breath away as we watched his mastery of heights where the oxygen would be too thin for us mere mortals.

And the view rendered me speechless!

Could anywhere be more beautiful on this earth? Our recent tedious and somewhat dangerous journey, with its accompanying disappointments, paled into insignificance at the sight of such a prize: the view from the summit.

When Paul wrote these words in Philippians chapter 3 he had already traversed a very difficult and dangerous path. He could have given up, gone home, complained of unfairness and injustice. Humanly speaking he had every right to do so, but the apostle knew that the promise of what lay ahead made the journey worthwhile.

God was calling Paul upward, and the twists and

disappointments of the difficult journey didn't stop him from reaching towards his final goal.

In pressing on, Paul gives us both the example and the encouragement to do the same... and the view from the top promises to be spectacular!

26

"Are not two sparrows sold for a copper coin? And not one of them falls to the ground apart from your Father's will. Do not fear therefore; you are of more value than many sparrows."

Matthew 10:29, 31

Recently I was captivated by a nature programme on television. A team of naturalists was exploring unknown jungle territory in South America, discovering species never before seen by man. They filmed huge tarantulas, observed endangered primates, fished in piranha-infested waters, avoided fearsome jaguars, and set up secret cameras to film, of all things, a wren's nest!

Imagine these high-flying nature experts spending time on this tiny little bird, which they could just as easily have studied in the UK! I was fascinated. What had caught their attention was the ability of this little bird to survive in such hostile territory, surrounded by so many predators.

Size does not equate with worth. In today's verses Jesus is explaining the importance of every part of God's creation. Sparrows are abundant in number, rather plain to look at, generally uninteresting as far as the bird world is concerned, and not of much monetary value either. In spite of all that, we are told that not *one* of them falls to the ground without God knowing about it. Wow!

In November 2011 the world's population was given as 7 billion. Does that make you feel small at all? It certainly does me.

Now, I wonder how many hairs that represents. Because in verse 30 of the same chapter Jesus reminds us that the very hairs of our head are numbered by God. It is information like this that helps me realize that our God is far greater than our puny little minds can imagine.

The prophet Isaiah, however, recognized exactly how big God is. He described God as the One who has "measured the waters in the hollow of His hand", and regarded the nations as "a drop in a bucket" (Isaiah 40:12, 15).

So remember today how awesome in power and glory God really is, and be blown away by the fact that this great God has stooped down in the form of His Son and by the presence of His Spirit to say to your heart: "Do not fear… you are of more value than many sparrows." And it is this very same God who is looking out for you!

27

"Yea, though I walk through the valley of the shadow of death, I will fear no evil; for You are with me; Your rod and Your staff, they comfort me."

Psalm 23:4

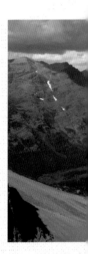

Grief is described in one dictionary as "a deep or intense sorrow". It seems such an unsatisfactory description of something that causes disruption of seismic proportions in our lives. Deep loss is usually its cause, especially the loss experienced because of the death of a loved one.

Psychologists can explain eloquently the various stages of grief – anger, denial, bargaining, depression, and acceptance – two of which, they say, must be visited before recovery can be expected.

Recovery becomes more of a problem when some people (perhaps even many) don't *experience* grief – they *live* in it. It becomes a place of abode, a place they need to be, a place of solitude, a place of guilt, regrets, sorrow and, amazingly, even a place of comfort.

I know this place, because I have lived there. After our first daughter died I held on to my grief for a long time. I felt that it was all I had left of her and that "normal" living would somehow be disrespectful, somehow make little of her death. Eventually I discovered that I was wrong – grief is not a place. We are not meant to stay there.

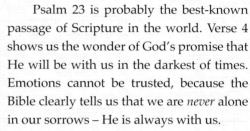

Psalm 23 is probably the best-known passage of Scripture in the world. Verse 4 shows us the wonder of God's promise that He will be with us in the darkest of times. Emotions cannot be trusted, because the Bible clearly tells us that we are *never* alone in our sorrows – He is always with us.

But there is one word in particular in this verse that fills me with great hope. It is the word "through". God promises to walk *through* the valley of the shadow of death with us – not stay with us in it. This is a journey – not a destination. In our deepest sorrow we need to recognize that there is a beginning and an end to grief, and the greatest of all companions walks with us between them.

For some the journey will take longer than for others, and I would not be as foolish as to say that sorrow will not be revisited. It will – but that is okay.

However, we do have cause to rejoice, because the One who has conquered death has promised to see us *through*… provided we leave our tent pegs at home!

28

"He has made everything beautiful in its time."

Ecclesiastes 3:11

The young woman in the delivery suite was creating mayhem. She was making delivery of her baby simply impossible: shouting, kicking, and even biting those of us gathered around her. Exhaustion and terror had set in, and absolutely nothing we said would calm her down. Hearing all the commotion, an older, senior midwife entered the room just as we were about to send for the anaesthetist.

During the very short space of time between contractions she took the young woman's face firmly in her hands. "Listen to me," she said, looking into her eyes. "In just a minute this pain is going to give you something beautiful, *so don't waste it* … use it! Now push!" Seconds later her beautiful baby girl was born, and her pain was already being filed away under "M" for memory.

I have never forgotten that piece of advice given by the wise midwife: "Don't waste your pain; instead use it, and it will produce something beautiful in your life." It works in exactly the same way for every situation in our lives too.

Pain is not something we willingly welcome in our lives. It is a force that can disable and destroy; it can cause despair and even devastation to the most secure individual; it can bring about change and uncertainty. Ultimately it leads to one of two conclusions: it can make us bitter or it can make us better.

I call Ecclesiastes 3 the "time chapter". It explains what we all know only too well: "To everything there is a season, a time for every purpose under heaven." In the chapter we read of happy times, sad times, and times of national disaster as well as personal difficulty. Life, as we know it, is all there, described in a few words.

Perhaps these words, like atheism, would make our existence seem rather pointless were it not for this wonderful promise in verse 11. Here, God promises to make "everything beautiful in its time".

Your heartache, your grief, your loneliness, your illness, your childlessness, your disappointment – whatever the source of your pain, God is able to use it to produce something beautiful in your life. Something that will bless the lives of others and bring glory to Him.

The old song by Gaither puts it so well:

All I had to offer Him was brokenness and strife,
But He made something beautiful of my life!

Extract taken from the song "Something Beautiful" by William J. Gaither/Gloria Gaither. Copyright © 1971 William J. Gaither, Inc. of Gaither Copyright Management

29

"I go to prepare a place for you. And if I go and prepare a place for you, I will come again and receive you to Myself; that where I am, there you may be also. And where I go you know, and the way you know."

John 14:2b–4

Hallelujah! This word loses its power in ink on paper. It needs to be shouted, or sung, or expressed in a way that can be felt. And the promise of Heaven makes me want to shout. It tugs at my heart, it gets me excited, it gives me a reason to go on.

Does it do that for you?

Many Christians seem to have little interest in Heaven – the ultimate promise of God – except perhaps when they need the thought of it as comfort during a time of bereavement. Even those of us who know we will spend *forever* there lack the excitement we should have.

We are off to Tenerife in two weeks' time for our summer holiday. I can't wait. I've never been before, yet already I have been on the internet, bought a travel guide, invested in some appropriate clothing for the hot weather, and quizzed some friends who know

what the place is like. And after all that investment in time and energy, do you know how long we are going for? A week – seven short days – and at this point I know more about Tenerife than many Christians know about the place from which they will never return!

Why is it, I wonder? Could it be because we follow this world's opinion of Heaven as a boring, airy-fairy place, lacking excitement and adventure? Perhaps we equate Heaven with some kind of dull church service that will go on and on… and on? Maybe it is because we don't like to think of death, and therefore we avoid taking the eternal perspective on life that every believer should have. Consequently we become earth-bound in our thinking, lacking effectiveness in our Christian lives, devoid of the knowledge of the amazing future that lies ahead.

If you are one of those who think that the Bible does not have much to say about Heaven, then I challenge you to look again. And when you have finished, add your "Hallelujah" to mine, in recognition of God's ultimate promise.

I can tell you this much: Tenerife won't hold a candle to it!

30

"The LORD is close to the brokenhearted; he rescues those whose spirits are crushed."

Psalm 34:18 (NLT)

There used to be an advertisement that showed a representation of a torn heart with a big sticking plaster across it, encouraging you to ask your doctor for a particular drug that might improve the health of your heart.

This picture of a sticking plaster trying to hold together a broken heart saddened me. If only broken hearts of another kind could be held together with something as simple.

As a nurse for over thirty years (much of it during the "troubles" in Belfast), I have been amazed at the wonder of modern medicine to put together human bodies that have literally been torn apart by bomb and bullet. I have watched patients affected by dreadful diseases helped on the road to partial, if not full, recovery.

The human body is indeed wonderfully resilient.

Those with a broken heart have less visible wounds that can prove more difficult to heal.

The "heart" is not merely a muscular blood pump; it is the seat of human emotion – the place of love, trust, and respect that we use in all of our human relationships. It is the intimate part of ourselves that we give to another, whether superficially in casual friendships, or deeply in our feelings towards family, and totally in the case of our life partner.

To be broken-hearted is to experience the emotional impact of another person's assault on all you have given them of yourself – whether it is intentional on their part or not. Love rejected, promises broken, abuse of body and mind, secrets revealed, dreams shattered; all of which leave a trail of emotional devastation that cannot easily be healed.

Yet in these verses hope rises once more for those who feel hurt, helpless, and hopeless. The psalmist promises that God is "close to the brokenhearted", and puts in motion a rescue plan for those who are crushed, whether by human design or unfortunate circumstances.

In fact the prophet Isaiah further explains to us in chapter 61:1 that one of the reasons Jesus was sent to this earth was "to heal the brokenhearted"; while Peter in his first letter encourages us to cast "all your care upon Him, for He cares for you" (5:7).

Why not reach out and share your heart with the One who will never break it? And He will not only heal it, He will give you the strength to live, love, and trust again.

31

"Come to Me, all you who labor and are heavy laden, and I will give you rest. Take My yoke upon you and learn from Me, for I am gentle and lowly in heart, and you will find rest for your souls."

Matthew 11:28–29

The "nurture or nature" debate has been rumbling on for many years. Is how we behave purely to do with the genetic data passed on by our parents? Does the genius displayed by a musician or scientist simply come from plenty of practise or study?

As I watch friends' children grow into adults there are times when I hear their mother's laugh, or I observe their father's walk in them. Is their behaviour due to genetics, or simply learned from spending so much time with these very significant people in their lives? It really doesn't matter. The point is they have become like them in different ways. They now display something of their parents' character.

In these beautiful verses Jesus demonstrates a number of things for our encouragement. First, He gives us an invitation to come to Him if we are weary and burdened by difficulty. Then

when we do, He promises us just what we need: rest!

But it is His follow-on request that intrigues me. Jesus, the Son of God, our Saviour, offers to "nurture" us in how to deal with the difficulties of life. It is almost as if He is saying: "Immediate rest is available for today's burdens, but if you spend time with Me, I can teach you how to live in perpetual rest."

That phrase "learn from Me" both touches and challenges my heart. The One who never fails to pick us up, dry our tears, listen to our groaning, and settle our troubled hearts wants to mentor us in order that we can become more like Him.

Just as the old ox is yoked together with the young beast in order that it might learn how to plough a straight furrow, so our Saviour wants not merely to walk beside us, but to be *connected* to us in order that we might learn how to live restful lives. Once in that partnership, Jesus has promised the kind of rest that this world can only dream of.

As Christians, our "nature" has now become that of children of God, by virtue of the new birth. But I wonder whether we spend enough time with the One who can "nurture" us, willingly connecting Himself to us in such a way that our burdens are lightened and our character is transformed.

The invitation of Jesus still stands: "Learn from Me… and you will find rest for your souls."

32

"I will instruct you and teach you in the way you should go; I will guide you with My eye."

Psalm 32:8

It was a very hot day as we joined the long queue at the bus stop for a trip to the market in the "must see" old town of Paphos. During our week-long break in Cyprus we had found travelling on public transport an amusing experience. The drivers all displayed a rather frenetic disposition, with hand-waving gestures, gruff facial expressions, and an ability to make you feel as though your presence was somehow spoiling their day!

Once on board the bus, clearly marked "Paphos Market", we sat back and enjoyed the trip as we left the trendy new harbour area and wound our way up through the steep, winding streets to the old town.

As we disembarked, one poor passenger dared to ask the direction of the market and was dismissed by a wave of the hand, with one finger pointing to the right. Like the proverbial "blind leading the blind" we all followed the leader of our little pack into the cobbled streets, and then off in various directions.

The town was completely deserted! Every shop was closed and coffee shops were locked up tight. Not a mortal soul was to be

seen – except for bemused tourists looking for the market. When we found the market area, guess what? It was also closed, displaying a sign in English which said: "Closed Monday for the public holiday"! Dejected, we headed back for the bus.

We had thought we knew where we were going and we even went in the right direction – and by a mode of transport that we presumed was trustworthy – but our journey was made pointless by a municipal authority running a service to nowhere!

Life can be a bit like that. We make our plans, perhaps even take advice, head in a direction that we think is right… only to discover we have been on the road to nowhere, and the resulting disappointment and frustration knocks us sideways.

How different things could be if we would learn the principles and experience the promise of these wise words from the psalmist.

Our heavenly Father is the One who wrote the manual on life, so there is no one better to go to for instruction. He sees down every path, so He is perfectly placed to guide us around, and sometimes through, difficult terrain. His plans do not include trickery, so we can trust His guidance, if we take the time to seek it.

And be assured: God never puts us on the road to nowhere!

33

"God sent forth His Son… to redeem… that we might receive the adoption as sons… and if a son, then an heir of God through Christ."

Galatians 4:4–5, 7

The little boy's short-term foster mother had gone to great lengths to prepare him for the future. "One day," she explained, "you are going to have a 'forever mummy and daddy' who will love you and look after you for all time."

And the promise for that little red-headed toddler came true when he was adopted by friends of ours. His excitement, happiness, delight, peace, and a multitude of other indescribable emotions, just tumble out of him when you are in his presence. You have to "speed" listen if you want to catch up with all his exciting news. He makes everyone smile.

This particular adopted son is now experiencing a new name and a new family. He knows on a daily basis what it means to be loved as never before. His future is secure, and his inheritance is sealed. He has received the ultimate in promises for a child – a happy home.

I have no idea what it is like to feel unloved; no idea what it is like to have a missing identity or to feel alone in this world; no idea of the devastation caused by abuse inflicted by someone who was meant to care. Yet I recognize that some understand only too well.

Even the image of a father figure is tainted by sin, and difficult for some to equate with what is good. However, the very best of earthly fathers cannot be compared to our heavenly Father. This

Father loves you so much that He wants to adopt you into His family, through redemption by His Son.

This Father will give you a new name, companionship for your loneliness, peace for your pain, an identity in the family of God, hope for the future, and an inheritance with His Son. Now that's a promise to make anyone smile.

And what's even more amazing: He doesn't do short-term. This is a "forever" relationship!

34

"Shall not the Judge of all the earth do right?"

Genesis 18:25

This sentence can be interpreted in different ways depending on where you place the emphasis. It can be read as a question requiring an answer, a rhetorical question, or a statement of promise. In context, it was rhetorical, as Abraham interceded with God over the judgement that was to fall on the wicked city of Sodom. He wanted God to treat the righteous "fairly" in that doomed place.

Fairness is one of those big issues that help us to accept or adjust to circumstances beyond our control. Something that smacks of unfairness or lack of justice causes hackles to rise and erects barriers to acceptance. It can be the seed that produces the destructive root of bitterness.

Yet in order to determine whether something is fair or not we need to be in possession of all the facts. We need to see things clearly from both sides.

Take the night our teenage son was about to leave the house for a night out with his friends. "Be back by 10 o'clock!" I shouted before he could escape.

Turning quickly he snapped: "That's not fair, Mum! John is allowed to stay out until 11 p.m. and David has a key – he can come in when he likes. That's just not fair!" His sense of injustice was reinforced by a stamp of the foot before he left.

Now, from where he was standing it wasn't fair, because his friends were allowed to do something he wasn't. But from where I was standing as his parent, and knowing the dangers that lurk in our streets late at night, it was more than fair – it was right.

Often we don't get to see the other side of the circumstances that cause us to question the "fairness" of God. He works on eternal perspectives, while we are hampered by only seeing things from a human viewpoint.

So the next time you want to stamp your foot and shout, "That's not fair, God!" picture your heavenly Father – the Judge of all the earth – across the room seeing the big picture and remember: He will only do what is right for you.

And that's a promise to blow away any clouds of doubt about the fairness of our God.

35

"He will quiet you with His love, He will rejoice over you with singing."

Zephaniah 3:17

My mother has always had a song for every occasion. Whether there was something to celebrate or merely the ordinary "to-dos" of every day it would be accompanied by a song.

A sunny day was welcomed with a cheery "The sun has got his hat on!", while a walk in the rain could produce a rendition of "I'm singing in the rain". My brother responded to Cliff Richard's hit song "Son, you'll be a bachelor boy" by marrying in his early twenties!

Songs for fun and songs for sorrow… we were blessed indeed with a loving family and a house filled with song.

While I don't have the same memory for lyrics as my mother, I have found both peace and joy in songs, especially those that minister God's word to my heart. Perhaps more singing was done in my own home in the dark recesses of the night than in daylight hours. When one of the girls was distressed, in pain or recovering from a seizure I would hold her close, gently stroking her temple, and sing to her of Jesus. I doubt it was the quality of my singing that quietened her, but rather the closeness of my presence and the depth of my love as we rocked together in the shadows.

I think it is the memories of those days, when my children needed me so much, that make these words from the prophecy of Zephaniah so precious in my life. Often in the turmoil of circumstances over which I had no control I experienced the reality of a loving heavenly Father.

When I didn't know where to turn, He was there. When my grief seemed enormous and inconsolable, He would whisper in my ear: "Catherine, I have loved you with an everlasting love" (see Jeremiah 31:3).

Undoubtedly, it was the closeness of His presence and the depth of His love that quietened my soul as we too rocked in the shadows together.

When Zephaniah broke fifty years of prophetic silence with God's message, the children of Israel were scattered and in exile. They were not only homeless and helpless, but also felt abandoned by the Lord Jehovah. Distress and despair were their daily companions.

But God had not forgotten them. Instead He gave them a message of hope and a declaration of His love through His prophet. With judgement now past, God would quiet them with His love, and *one day* rejoice over them with singing.

What a joy to know that the promise still stands. If we stay close enough for His embrace, He will quiet us with His love. And one day, as part of His redeemed bride, He will rejoice over us with singing!

36

"Be strong and of good courage; do not be afraid, nor be dismayed, for the LORD your God is with you wherever you go."

Joshua 1:9b

Moses, the great leader of the children of Israel, was dead. The task ahead was huge, the resources were few. How would this motley horde of nomadic tribesmen ever be able to conquer Canaan? Joshua, as Moses' right-hand man, knew they were often questioning, complaining, and easily distracted if the way ahead looked tough. There wasn't a general alive who would anticipate victory with this army!

But Joshua's confidence did not lie in people or in armies. Instead, he knew victory was secure because of his Colonel-in-Chief. His supreme Commander had got them this far, and in doing so had proved to Joshua that He was a promise-keeping God.

As Joshua faced the biggest task of his life, God saw his fear, and responded with a promise – not once, but three times (verses 6–7, 9). To the Hebrews, threefold repetition indicated the highest degree of emphasis. In essence God was saying to Joshua, "My commitment to you is not in doubt. I will be with you every step of the way."

Joshua would be let down by people, discouraged by circumstances, deceived by individuals, and disappointed by progress, but never, never, never abandoned by God. And that promise sustained him through the battle and gave him victory after victory.

Those in Christian leadership today face all of the above as they engage in spiritual warfare. Whether leading a church, a Sunday school class, a youth organization, a small study group, a worship group... whatever and wherever makes no difference.

Perhaps the situation seems hopeless, or the task ahead impossible? I encourage you to take time out and listen once more to the "repeated" promise of God:

Be strong, courageous, fearless and undismayed... for the Lord your God is with you wherever you go!

37

"Everyone who competes in the games goes into strict training. They do it to get a crown that will not last; but we do it to get a crown that will last for ever."

1 Corinthians 9:25 (NIV)

Were you watching the 2012 London Olympic Games – where we in Britain saw Team GB win more medals than ever before? Weren't the athletes amazing? There was a myriad of sports most of us only see once every four years: swimming, cycling, sailing, running and… rowing! The rowing competition in particular got us Coleraine folk buzzing, as we followed three young local men in their bid for Olympic success. They did us proud, winning medals to prove it: two silver ones, quickly backed up by a hard-earned bronze.

Prior to the event, a special documentary programme had shown the strict daily training these guys were involved in to prepare for their individual events. The intense discipline and pain they put themselves through, in order to be at their very best, was jaw-dropping to watch. The cold, dark, early morning runs; muscle-stretching weight training; strict dietary control; mile after lonely mile pulling on oars. All three rowers continued with dogged determination, day after day for four years, until they reached that unforgettable moment when they stood on the winners' podium.

Now that's what I call commitment. Yet each of those young men would tell you that the result was worth every uncomfortable minute, the reward for ultimate sporting success being truly great: a medal, the applause of their peers, and the admiration of the world… for a short time at least. I genuinely take my hat off to them.

In this verse, however, the apostle is speaking of promised rewards for those of us who follow Jesus as Saviour. Our salvation has been accomplished purely by the work of Christ on the cross for us; it has nothing to do with personal achievement, yet for every believer there is the promised prize of Heaven itself; while other eternal rewards are at God's discretion depending on how we have served Him on earth.

There may be times when we feel like giving up, but we are encouraged to keep on running in this "race"; to live disciplined lives; to stay focused on Christ; to be committed to *daily* training in righteousness, remembering that the finishing tape is within reach and the award ceremony ahead!

38

"We desire… that you do not become sluggish, but imitate those who through faith and patience inherit the promises."

Hebrews 6:11–12

It was September 2000, and having just said goodbye to our son at the Royal College of Music "halls", we started on the long journey home to Northern Ireland. Pulling into a petrol station to obtain the necessary fuel, my husband said: "I'll only get half a tank here, and we can fill up outside London, where it'll be cheaper." I remember thinking that made sense. Little did I know how foolish that action was going to seem in a few hours' time!

We were shocked to see cars queued right down the road as we passed a petrol station on our way into Oxford. Then a radio news bulletin told us what we didn't want to hear – the UK was gripped in an all-out petrol strike!

Rebuking ourselves for not filling up when we had the chance, we were still convinced that surely we would be able to get petrol *somewhere* between Oxford and Holyhead in North Wales.

But it was not to be. Station after station was sold out. We travelled across Anglesey to the ferry, with the fuel warning light glowing red and the car propelled by fumes and prayer! We were running on empty.

As Christians, too many of us "run on empty". We never seem to take on board enough spiritual fuel for our journey. Some even try to make it on "fumes" alone, thinking that opening their Bible once a week at church will help get them through until the next time. Such behaviour leaves us without power to live a godly life in this ungodly world.

It also deprives us of experiencing the promises of God. The writer to the Hebrews pleads with us not to become lazy, but rather to copy those men and women whose faith and patience lead to receiving the promises of God.

Take heart: God never goes on strike! So if you are feeling empty and powerless, why not ditch laziness and head for God's word? The time you spend there will be rewarded with all that you need. And the promises of God are added in abundance!

39

"And be kind to one another, tenderhearted, forgiving one another, even as God in Christ forgave you."

Ephesians 4:32

The whimpering was coming from the third bed on the left. The young IRA man didn't look so brave now as he lay in the dim light of the ward, both of his knees shattered in a so-called punishment shooting, drips and drains confining him to the bed.

As a young nurse working in a major Belfast hospital I had learned not to ask questions, but rather to treat every patient in exactly the same way. Politics had no place in medical care. It wasn't always easy, especially during the republican feud that was filling our surgical wards at that time.

And so night after night I looked after him as best I could, nursing his wounds and spending time talking to him when he was overcome with fear, trying not to think what injury he might have inflicted on others. As each night of my week-long shift pattern passed the young man made steady improvement towards physical recovery.

Returning to day duty after a few days off, I was delighted to see him walking down the ward towards me on crutches. "You're on your feet!" I exclaimed. But my smile was not returned.

"Why didn't you tell me you were one of *them*?" he snarled, aggressively pushing his face into mine. The next few minutes were heartbreaking as he gushed abuse at me.

"I'm not here as a Protestant," I replied nervously. "I'm here as a nurse."

With oaths and curses he headed back to his bed, unable to forgive me for the place or religion of my birth. Now well enough to allow hate to become his master once more, he never spoke to me again.

Forgiveness is hard – whatever the situation. Sometimes people wrong us dreadfully, inflicting wounds of all kinds. Other times we *feel* wronged simply because of what someone stands for. Our sinful nature cries out: "Vengeance!"

Our Saviour, from the cross, cried out: "Father, forgive them!"

Yes, forgiveness is hard, but it is also healing and liberating. Ephesians 4:32 may not at first glance appear to be a promise, but in its outworking it promises more than we may ever realize.

The words on a poster in our church hall explain it beautifully: "When you forgive, you set a prisoner free… and then you discover the prisoner was you!"

91

40

"Joseph said to them, 'Do not be afraid, for am I in the place of God?... you meant evil against me; but God meant it for good...'"

Genesis 50:19–20a

The story of Joseph is certainly the stuff of blockbusters. Within the relevant chapters of the book of Genesis is contained the true story of a dysfunctional family: sibling rivalry, domestic violence, human trafficking, slavery, imprisonment, and a happy ending!

Joseph's future had looked bright as the father's favourite son. He would never be in want, and would always know the love and security of his family home and business. That is until one day when everything started to go wrong. Aged only seventeen, he went through a series of tragic events that turned his world upside down – all initiated by his own brothers! Everything he had that was good was taken away from him.

Except, that is, his trust in God.

During the succeeding years God took Joseph and changed him from an arrogant, spoiled young man into a wise and trusted leader. Along the way Joseph experienced hurt, disappointment, loneliness, and fear. He had plenty of time to plan some kind of payback for what his brothers had done to him, yet his growth was

not merely in character but also in godliness.

When Joseph eventually got to meet his brothers again he was able to forgive them because of what he had learned from God. He could see that all the evil that had been planned against him was in fact turned into good by God, in order that His greater plan for humanitarian aid for Egypt and the surrounding nations could be worked out. Multitudes were saved from famine because of Joseph.

We often look at personal disasters in our own lives as evil. It seems impossible that anything good could come out of our difficulties, our disappointments, our pain. We may go as far as to say that God couldn't possibly be in any of these things.

Yet in this statement of Joseph we see a beautiful promise: "God meant it for good."

If your world is falling apart right now, please draw strength and hope from these words of promise. One day the apparent evil in your life will show evidence of a loving, merciful God who only has your good at heart.

Take it from one who has experienced it – God means it for good!

Catherine Campbell's website is:
www.catherine-campbell.com.

It provides details of her forthcoming speaking engagements, and information about her other books.

You can also find Catherine on Facebook!

Picture Acknowledgments

Alison Hickey: pp. 33, 65, 71, 79, 93

Corbis: p. 13 Sean Justice; p. 25 Christopher Talbot Frank; p. 29 Vince Cavataio/Design Pics; p. 35 Carl Shaneff/Design Pics; p. 37 Hal Beral/ Visuals Unlimited; p. 43 Paul Souders; p. 54 Philip Lee Harvey/cultura; p. 57 Jamie Grill; p. 77 AStock; p. 87 Pete Saloutos/Blend Images; p. 89 Heide Benser; p. 91 Luca Da Ros/SOPA RF/SOPA

Debbie Willer: pp. 19, 53, 60, 67, 72, 85

Estelle Lobban: p. 68

Frans Mosca: pp. 27, 49

Jean Picton: pp. 9, 39, 47, 58, 82, 96

Len Kerswill: pp. 11, 16, 63, 81

Roger Chouler: pp. 5, 15, 21, 23, 30, 41, 44, 45, 51, 75, 95